TOUGH TIME, NICE TIME

Ridiculusmus

TOUGH TIME, NICE TIME

OBERON BOOKS
LONDON

First published in 2008 by Oberon Books Ltd
521 Caledonian Road, London N7 9RH
Tel: 020 7607 3637 / Fax: 020 7607 3629
e-mail: info@oberonbooks.com
www.oberonbooks.com

A catalogue record for this book is available from the British
Library.

ISBN: 978-1-84002-831-7

Characters

MARTIN REINHARDT: A Bangkok resident in his 40s

STEFAN THIERACK: A man in his late 30s from Hamburg

Setting: A sauna in Bangkok

Tough time, nice time was first performed by Ridiculusmus at the Pit Theatre in the Barbican Centre, London on 13 February 2008, with the following cast:

MARTIN, Jon Haynes
STEFAN, David Woods

Created by David Woods & Jon Haynes
Designed by Jon Haynes, Mischa Twitchin and David Woods
Lighting by Mischa Twitchin

Production Manager Ian Brown
Production Researcher Elena Timplalexi
Producer Sarah Greentree
General Manager Joanna Crowley

Thanks to all at the Melbourne Fringe Festival; Michael Kantor; Jeremy Hardingham and the Judith E. Wilson Drama Studio and Cambridge University English Department; Gideon Lester at Harvard University and Rob Orchard at the American Repertory Theatre; David Jubb, Richard Dufty, Luke Girling and all at BAC; Karl Wallace and all at the Belltable Arts, Claudia Woolger at The Source Arts Centre, Joe Murphy at St Johns Arts Centre, Listowel, The Mason Arms Derry, John Burns; Natalie Querol, Caroline Routh, The Empty Space and Northern Stage; Shunt; Gregory Nash and The Point; Greg Piggot & David Harradine; David Hardcastle; Phil Tragen; Emma Green; Rosie Mortimer; Sarah Jane Rawlings; Nicola Conibere; Rose Cobbe at United Agents; Pasit Sukrussameenuttakun, Chakorn Rassameephauengphou, Sathit Sirinadcharoen, Stefanie Huter, Reinhardt Hagen, Stefan Herold, Patrizia Paolini, Meredith Davies, Pascale Gillet, Babylon in Bangkok; Hannah Bentley, Louise Jeffreys, Angela Dias, Victoria Stiles, Liz Littlewood, Katie Filder, Sarah Shaw, Simon Bourne, Kate Beard and all at the Barbican; Sanjit Sil and Arts Council England; Kate, Louis and Stan.

Tough time, nice time

MARTIN: *Brokeback Mountain.* You seen that one?

STEFAN: Yeah, I cry my eyes out.

MARTIN: I thought it was shit.

STEFAN: No, I didn't cry my eyes out.

MARTIN: Last good movie I saw was –

STEFAN: My friend – she cried her eyes out.

MARTIN: *Just like Heaven…*you seen it?

STEFAN: No, but…I saw *Walk the Line…Walk the Line.*

MARTIN: I didn't see that. I saw *Munich.*

STEFAN: Oh that's on now. Is that worth seeing?

MARTIN: No…it's shit.

STEFAN: You know the documentary? *One Day in September*? Because my father was in the army then – he was on the roof eating hamburgers.

MARTIN: Really?

STEFAN: Yes, he was one of the fat bastards. And my grandfather was in the SS. He was Einsatzgruppen, cleaning up the Jews from the Polish border. Did you know that?

MARTIN: I didn't know that. My family weren't Nazi.

STEFAN: They were just ordinary Germans?

MARTIN: Ordinary Germans. But my grandparents kept some Russians on the farm as pigs. Forced them to live like pigs on their farm.

STEFAN: Were they Jews?

MARTIN: No, just Russians.

STEFAN: Russian Jews?

MARTIN: Maybe. I tell you I've got so many stories, Stefan.

STEFAN: Yeah, tell me, tell me stories. Why they keep them as pigs?

MARTIN: I need someone to write my stories for me, make them into a book.

STEFAN: Why?

MARTIN: I can't write.

STEFAN: Why don't you talk them into the machine? And employ an audio typist –

MARTIN: I need someone to write it for me, because I couldn't put it in words on a page.

STEFAN: Yes, but why do you want them in words on a page?

MARTIN: Because.

STEFAN: Because what?

MARTIN: Just wait, okay, wait and see. You'll find out.

STEFAN: Okay…so I could write for you…I could write it all down and you speak.

MARTIN: You ever heard about someone waiting for the police to come while a guy bleeds to death before him on the floor?

STEFAN: Yeah.

MARTIN: Me, happened to me.

STEFAN: Really?

MARTIN: You heard a guy comes back one day to his condominium – he's sharing with someone else – finds everything gone. Computer, valuables, TV, all gone, bare?

STEFAN: You?

MARTIN: Happened to me.

Pause.

Maybe you're not the right person.

STEFAN: You can try.

MARTIN: Hmm?

STEFAN: You can try. I can give them back to you.

MARTIN: But I don't want to tell you if…then you might do something with them and –

STEFAN: I can write them for you and give them back to you.

MARTIN: Maybe you steal them.

STEFAN: I can type in front of you and just… I can type them on a typewriter and give the pages to you as they come out.

MARTIN: I'm not sure I trust you.

STEFAN: I just want to help you.

MARTIN: Not sure I trust you.

STEFAN: Why not?

MARTIN: I know nothing about you

STEFAN: What do you want to know? What do you need to make you relax?

MARTIN: Huh?

STEFAN: I tell the story of my father –

MARTIN: Sex.

STEFAN: – in the SS and – what?

MARTIN: – if we like the same thing.

STEFAN: Look, I tell the story of my father in the SS and you tell me your story.

MARTIN: Yes, but I can do nothing with your story.

STEFAN: You can, you can take it and you can steal it.

MARTIN: Yes, but I can't write it.

STEFAN: Why not? Why can't you write my story if I can write your story?

MARTIN: I can't write.

STEFAN: You could remember and then tell it to someone else.

MARTIN: Alright, so tell me your story.

STEFAN: No, you start your one about the blood.

MARTIN: You first.

STEFAN: But you have two stories and I have only one good one, so you tell one first.

MARTIN: No, you first.

STEFAN: As a down payment.

MARTIN: No.

STEFAN: Of your story.

MARTIN: No.

STEFAN: And then I tell mine and you tell the other one.

MARTIN: No, I don't trust you.

STEFAN: Then we can't continue. This is the end of the conversation.

MARTIN: Alright. Boring.

STEFAN: Yeah. Shits happen. I was looking forward to your story. 'Specially the one about the guy –

MARTIN: It's your fault.

STEFAN: – having all the possessions taken from his flat, sounds really fun.

MARTIN: Yeah.

STEFAN: It was you…what have you done?

MARTIN: Hmm?

STEFAN: Does somebody not like you so much? So why have they got this against you?

MARTIN: I done nothing, they were just criminal.

STEFAN: Well where's the story in that?

MARTIN: I gave them my trust.

STEFAN: You let these people use your flat.

MARTIN: I let them use my condominium.

STEFAN: Yes.

MARTIN: They can stay there.

STEFAN: And then they just took everything?

MARTIN: I spoke to their family.

STEFAN: Why don't you…

MARTIN: I trusted them, I thought they were trustworthy.

STEFAN: …go to their family and ask them.

MARTIN: They've all disappeared.

STEFAN: Everybody disappeared?

MARTIN: I spoke to them on the phone, now they don't answer the phone.

STEFAN: So you need some money?

MARTIN: No, I'm a lawyer, I don't need money.

STEFAN: Oh, yeah, you're lawyer.

MARTIN: Hmm?

STEFAN: Your whole family are lawyers I suppose.

MARTIN: No.

STEFAN: Lots of money.

MARTIN: You?

STEFAN: Told you, publishing,

MARTIN: Yes, good?

STEFAN: What, for money?

MARTIN: Well, for anything.

STEFAN: It's all right, you know.

MARTIN: Keep you satisfied?

STEFAN: I'm not satisfied.

MARTIN: Well do something else then.

STEFAN: No, I like doing what I'm doing. It gives me something to moan about.

MARTIN: But?

STEFAN: But I'm not satisfied.

MARTIN: Yes, haven't I seen you before?

STEFAN: Well I arrived on Monday on the Lufthansa…

MARTIN: About two years…two years ago no?

STEFAN: I have been before.

MARTIN: Yes, about two years ago, in Lumpini Park View I saw you lying on a sofa, this guy's condominium, no?

STEFAN: Highly possible.

MARTIN: Your condominium.

STEFAN: Can't remember.

MARTIN: You were there.

STEFAN: Can't remember a moment of it.

MARTIN: I think you were off your face.

STEFAN: Usually.

MARTIN: At the time.

STEFAN: Usually I am.

MARTIN: Saying 'When are the poppers going to arrive?' It was you, no?

STEFAN: Did I say that?

MARTIN: I'm sure it was you.

STEFAN: As if some sort of delivery bird was coming with my nightly need. No, I'm in publishing, ghost writing, that sort of thing, but my father was in the SS.

MARTIN: So you keep saying.

STEFAN: No, my grandfather was in the SS. My father was in the German police, during the crisis in Munich in 1972.

MARTIN: So tell me the story…your father.

STEFAN: In Munich?

MARTIN: Israeli police.

STEFAN: Yes, eating the hamburgers while the Israelis were being shot in the flat by the Palestinians.

MARTIN: Really.

STEFAN: It's all in the story, big films, *Munich*, *One Day in September*, you've seen them all.

MARTIN: No but *Munich*'s not all about that.

STEFAN: Oh it's not?

MARTIN: It's about the aftermath.

STEFAN: Ah.

MARTIN: It's not. It's inspired by real events, which they can't prove, I think.

STEFAN: Tom Hanks?

MARTIN: He's not in it…he's in *Da Vinci Code*, which is being subjected to a lawsuit now.

STEFAN: Dan Brown.

MARTIN: Yes, but the authors of the book *The Holy Blood and the Holy Grail* are suing him, theft of their idea.

STEFAN: Is it…

MARTIN: You know this story?

STEFAN: No…is it in his book as well?

MARTIN: What?

STEFAN: The thing he's stolen.

MARTIN: Yeah, the story is the story of *The Da Vinci Code*, which I haven't read, is the same story that's in the book *The Holy Blood and the Holy Grail*…you haven't read this book? Nor have I. It's about the theory that Jesus married Mary Magdalen and they had a child. That's his mother, no?

STEFAN: No, Mary.

MARTIN: Yes, Magdalen.

STEFAN: Mary Magdalen was a prostitute who Jesus –

MARTIN: Not his mother?

STEFAN: No…Jesus took –

MARTIN: Who was his mother then? She was also Mary. Confused.

STEFAN: Not. She is the character the Catholics worship –

MARTIN: Oh, Catholics.

STEFAN: – as if she was a god…

MARTIN: Anyway, the story is…

STEFAN: Are you a Catholic?

MARTIN: No, I'm nothing. Story is…

STEFAN: I too, I am Socialist.

MARTIN: Are you listening to what I'm telling you?

STEFAN: Yes.

MARTIN: The story is…*Holy Blood and the Holy Grail*, Dan Brown uses this story, but his defence is that it's not these people's idea anyway, it's common knowledge, notion, this idea.

STEFAN: Yes.

MARTIN: So he's giving nothing. These…

STEFAN: Yes.

MARTIN: It's like stealing the story of Noah's Ark or Robin Hood.

STEFAN: *The Epic of Gilgamesh.*

MARTIN: Exactly.

STEFAN: So same as the *Life of Pi.*

MARTIN: But we digress from *Munich.* Anyway.

STEFAN: Yeah, so afterwards, after the killing.

MARTIN: After the kidnappers…the hostages had all been killed. The President of Israel, who was Mrs Golda Meir, I think, at the time, called a meeting in her home, and this is in the movie, and they, er, resolve to find and kill, all the people, all the Palestinians – is it? – who planned the kidnapping, the whole thing, and over the next five to ten years eleven of the thirteen who organised the whole thing were killed all round the world, they'd gone frantically *bah-bah-bah-bah-bah*, all dead, and the movie just shows that.

STEFAN: So the last two, where are they?

MARTIN: Don't know, can't remember…it tells you in the credits and I've forgotten.

STEFAN: It is you and I.

Pause.

It is us.

MARTIN: Well, that would be a good story, no?

STEFAN: Do we have to pay someone for that or…

MARTIN: What? The story?

STEFAN: Can we pretend it is you and I that are the last two unkilled German –

MARTIN: No, you just thought of it.

STEFAN: German-based Palestinians.

MARTIN: Why, you just thought of it.

STEFAN: Maybe somebody thought of it before like *Full Monty* or *Life of Pi.*

MARTIN: *The Full Monty*? Someone else thought of that?

STEFAN: Yah.

MARTIN: Really. Mmm.

STEFAN: There was some stage show which the idea for the film was stolen from.

MARTIN: And *Life of Pi*?

STEFAN: *Life of Pi* also was stolen from somebody else.

MARTIN: Is a good movie, *Life of Pi*?

STEFAN: No. It's a man on a raft with a panther or a tiger.

MARTIN: Sounds like a kid's tale.

STEFAN: Yes it's a fable but it is the winner of the Booker Prize, which means it must be good to read when you are in a cash and carry supermarket.

Pause.

MARTIN: What are we talking about?

STEFAN: You were going to tell me your story and we spoke of the ownership of stories and the films we liked and we spoke…we didn't speak, but I wanted to say something about the death of Ariel Sharon.

MARTIN: Is he dead?

STEFAN: He's on a life support machine.

MARTIN: He's not dead.

STEFAN: Practically dead and I saw…you know how this celebrity rubbish fills the papers and you see that 'Tom is not in love anymore with Angelina'.

MARTIN: Tom Cruise?

STEFAN: Whoever it may be.

MARTIN: Tom Hanks?

STEFAN: It may be, I don't know, I don't follow it, and then 'Paul and Heather get together again', and then I saw this other one – 'Sharon has a last chance…', and I thought oh, who is this Sharon? It must be Sharon – you know, Sharon Stone or something.

MARTIN: Oh I see, very funny.

STEFAN: And I read it and it's Ariel Sharon. But it's because we are so exposed to this celebrity shit I thought it was a celebrity called Sharon and not the President of Israel. Now tell your fucking story.

MARTIN: I told you it, I told you the story already.

STEFAN: Not the story of the man with the blood.

MARTIN: That's it, I told you.

STEFAN: That's it? Some guy with blood slashed his –

MARTIN: Some guy in my condominium.

STEFAN: Slashed you on the face and then died as you rang an ambulance, and did you leave a bloody mess on the carpet?

MARTIN: Me?

STEFAN: Was there a mess on the carpet?

MARTIN: Course there was…someone bleeds to death in your condominium, what you think?

STEFAN: Do you have tiles or a carpet?

MARTIN: Tiles.

STEFAN: Yes?

MARTIN: With runners.

STEFAN: So you wash it off afterwards and just throw the rugs.

MARTIN: I had to throw the rugs away.

STEFAN: So what was wrong with him?

MARTIN: Unbalanced.

STEFAN: You were looking after him? Taking care of him? You wanted to help?

MARTIN: Hmm?

STEFAN: You wanted to help.

MARTIN: Me?

STEFAN: Yes.

MARTIN: At the beginning.

STEFAN: First you wanted to help.

MARTIN: Then it became like a leech in my side.

STEFAN: And then he just slashed his body and your face.

MARTIN: Tried to throw himself off the balcony –

STEFAN: Yeah?

MARTIN: – as well.

STEFAN: You stopped that?

MARTIN: It was just a cry for help, he wouldn't have done it.

STEFAN: So you just watched him attempt –

MARTIN: Till he gave up, got bored with –

STEFAN: Was it funny?

MARTIN: Lack of attention.

STEFAN: Was it funny?

MARTIN: Quite funny.

STEFAN: Yeah, yeah, I like to see some people do the attempt at suicide as a cry for help but it goes wrong and they actually die…or better still they do the attempt of suicide as the cry for help get it wrong and end up brain damaged or physically backward.

MARTIN: Funny.

STEFAN: Yeah, yeah, yeah, yeah, like a cabbage or something…and another good one are the woman from

Thailand who cames to America in order to have some bowel operation because she had bad hospital treatment in Thailand ended up as a side result she had bowel cancer so she cames to America thinking oh they look after me in this lovely place, my sister is there, they pay 30,000 Dollars for the operation in a private hospital…put her under anaesthetic, lock her in a room on a monitor and then for some reason she blacks out and they don't notice that she has no air coming into her and then when –

MARTIN: She dies?

STEFAN: No when they realise she has no air, they see through the door but they can't get through the door because someone else has locked it, they can't find the key, change of shift, security protocol and so forth…and it takes fifteen minutes for them to get through the door and by this time she has no oxygen to the brain and she is a cabbage and although she is alive, she doesn't recognise herself, her family, her son. Her son says, she doesn't know who I am…but…at least she hasn't got bowel cancer.

MARTIN: You find that funny.

STEFAN: Yes.

MARTIN: Hmm.

STEFAN: Because you know, Martin, I like to see people suffer, it gives me great pleasure. And you also?

MARTIN: No.

STEFAN: So you don't understand *Schadenfreude*?

MARTIN: No.

STEFAN: You know what it is?

MARTIN: No.

STEFAN: But you don't understand *Schadenfreude*?

MARTIN: Yes, don't understand.

STEFAN: You don't understand the pleasure in seeing someone suffer? Or you don't want to admit it?

MARTIN: No.

STEFAN: Why not?

MARTIN: Well why do you?

STEFAN: Because it makes me feel good. It makes feel very good, I feel fine and this person has just walked into a lamppost.

MARTIN: No, I don't get that feeling.

STEFAN: You have laughed at Mr Bean walking into a lamppost?

MARTIN: I don't find him funny.

STEFAN: But you have laughed.

MARTIN: No.

STEFAN: At somebody falling over. Tripping on a banana skin? A clown?

MARTIN: Probably.

STEFAN: You have probably laughed at a clown.

MARTIN: Yes maybe, maybe.

STEFAN: Definitely have.

MARTIN: Well what about it? Doesn't mean I want people to suffer.

STEFAN: Yes but this is *Schadenfreude.*

MARTIN: It's only pretend.

STEFAN: You have seen the *Schadenfreude.*

MARTIN: But I don't laugh at someone turning into a cabbage.

STEFAN: Okay so imagine this…if you had the power to cut off someone's head with an axe, no guilt, no problem, you want to try it?

MARTIN: No.

STEFAN: What if I said 'If you don't do this I kill you'?

MARTIN: No thanks.

STEFAN: So I kill you?

MARTIN: Huh?

STEFAN: You rather I kill you than you just chop off someone's head?

MARTIN: No.

STEFAN: No guilt, no problem.

MARTIN: It's not the choice.

STEFAN: Come.

MARTIN: You're talking hypothetically.

STEFAN: Come to Rwanda, we can do it tomorrow –

MARTIN: There's no problem there now.

STEFAN: Yes it's in Burundi now.

MARTIN: Bollocks.

STEFAN: Yes this is it right, we fly –

MARTIN: I'm not flying to Burundi now.

STEFAN: No you can't fly to Burundi, but say we stay at Hotel Milles Collines in…err, I forget the name of the place – Kigali, okay, no, so say we fly to Nairobi, take an overland trip to Burundi – tie up with some Angolan rebels –

MARTIN: You're talking rubbish.

STEFAN: – and we say we just want to kill someone, just for the fun –

MARTIN: I don't want to kill someone just for the fun.

STEFAN: We have US Dollars.

MARTIN: It doesn't give me fun, taking life.

STEFAN: Yah – you see the blood.

MARTIN: Don't want to see blood.

STEFAN: You see the soul.

MARTIN: No thanks, I've seen it already on film.

STEFAN: That's actors.

MARTIN: I've seen real on film.

STEFAN: Who have you seen real on film?

MARTIN: I've seen footage.

STEFAN: Israelis?

MARTIN: Yeah, this kind of thing.

STEFAN: And you like it?

MARTIN: No.

STEFAN: And then why you watch?

MARTIN: Hmm?

STEFAN: You want to see a snuff movie?

MARTIN: Morbid curiosity.

STEFAN: So you like it?

MARTIN: No, I switch it off.

STEFAN: You go to cinema, you invest money, you like it.

MARTIN: When are you going to listen to me? I told you I have all these stories.

STEFAN: I'm listening, I'm ready, so tell me now.

MARTIN: Just give me a call, okay? Give me a call.

STEFAN: I tell you now, I have a pen. I have a book.

MARTIN: Give me a call. They're not – I tell you, I promise you, they're not money-boy stories. They're not stories of money-boys.

STEFAN: Yes, I don't want stories of money-boys.

MARTIN: If you want stories of money-boys you go ask these guys. They're not this kind of thing. Boring. And they're not stories of money-boys.

STEFAN: Tell me the truth.

MARTIN: Mmm?

STEFAN: Tell me the truth as you know it.

MARTIN: The truth?

STEFAN: Yeah.

MARTIN: Look in the mirror. Cute guy, hmm?

STEFAN: Me? You?

MARTIN: You. Cute guy.

STEFAN: So what is this story?

MARTIN: Okay, I'll tell you the story, but give me a call.

STEFAN: No, I'm telling you now, I'm ready. It's too good to wait for.

MARTIN: Give me a call. Not here, okay, I told you we have dinner, we have sauna, we take an evening over it –

STEFAN: Okay –

MARTIN: And then you tell me – I tell you what it's about, and you tell me if you are interested.

STEFAN: Okay.

MARTIN: You just tell me if you're interested, because maybe it doesn't interest you. You tell me. When I tell you what it's about you say interested or not interested –

STEFAN: Okay, so when do you want?

MARTIN: – and then we can proceed. I don't want money, okay?

STEFAN: When do you want dinner, yeah?

MARTIN: One night this – give me a call. One night this week, okay?

STEFAN: Why do you keep doing that? You're just dangling, teasing –

MARTIN: I told you, I've got business to do – I –

STEFAN: Why you say things when you don't mean them?

MARTIN: Mean which things?

STEFAN: You don't trust me?

MARTIN: I don't know what I do.

STEFAN: You said you trusted me and you were going to tell me good stories.

MARTIN: Yes.

STEFAN: So why aren't you telling them?

MARTIN: Okay, I'm a lawyer, and I sell ecstasy.

STEFAN: Yeah, well look –

MARTIN: So I'm a busy man. Could be tomorrow – if you call me tomorrow I may be free, may be not.

STEFAN: What are you doing now? Where are you going now?

MARTIN: Oh, I go to eat at Sizzler now.

STEFAN: Well why don't we eat together at Sizzler?

MARTIN: You like Sizzler?

STEFAN: Yeah.

MARTIN: At CP Tower? You come with me now?

STEFAN: You can tell me, yeah.

MARTIN: Okay, we go to Sizzler, we eat in Sizzler, okay? Did you hear someone tried to poison it? The other week? Someone tried to poison Sizzler?

STEFAN: No.

MARTIN: They lost billions of dollars in a few hours. They had to close all salad bars. Someone put rat pellets in the salad bar, you know? You hear about this?

STEFAN: What, in the bacon bits?

MARTIN: In Sydney and in Bangkok, it happened. Lost billions of dollars in two hours. Closed salad bars. Some kind of nut. Rat pellets in the salad bar.

STEFAN: In Sydney and Bangkok?

MARTIN: Mmm? Millions of dollars in two hours.

STEFAN: Which one was it?

MARTIN: Which one? There's only two in Bangkok.

STEFAN: So?

MARTIN: Three Sizzler in Sydney.

STEFAN: Which one had the rat poison?

MARTIN: All of them.

STEFAN: So there must be more than one nut then if they can do it in Sydney and Bangkok.

MARTIN: Yes. I think not at the same time.

STEFAN: A team of nutters, yeah?

MARTIN: Maybe. I think they don't know yet.

STEFAN: So somebody from Sydney comes to Bangkok.

MARTIN: Yes.

STEFAN: With the rat poison.

MARTIN: Yes, yes.

STEFAN: Flies back to Sydney with more rat poison.

MARTIN: Yes. Anyway, so you want to hear the stories? I liked what you said before. Maybe you can turn it into a novel.

STEFAN: Yeah that would be brilliant.

MARTIN: I don't – whatever happens, don't mention my name, okay?

STEFAN: Why, what is it?

MARTIN: Martin.

STEFAN: No, your surname.

MARTIN: Why d'you want to know?

STEFAN: When you're famous your surname becomes redundant, but as you're not yet I thought –

MARTIN: What's yours?

STEFAN: Thierack.

MARTIN: Hmm?

STEFAN: Did you not hear me?

MARTIN: Don't understand.

STEFAN: What is there to understand? It's a simple enough name. Thierack, as in Otto George.

MARTIN: He's your what? Your father?

STEFAN: My grandfather. No I'm just saying the name is the same. But yeah he…we are probably related. He had these eight iron hooks…many people who were not actually guilty were strung up on iron hooks. You can see them still if you go to Plötzensee prison, they still have the –

MARTIN: People? Hanging up?

STEFAN: No, the iron hooks with the blood stains on the walls.

MARTIN: Blood stains still there?

STEFAN: Yeah.

MARTIN: You've been?

STEFAN: Yeah, yeah always I've been. I've been to Nürnberg, I've seen the trial courtrooms. I think it's important.

MARTIN: Yes?

STEFAN: You know, to see what has happened in the history and –

MARTIN: Yes, well we all know.

STEFAN: So that perhaps you know it doesn't happen again and also it's quite a good laugh.

MARTIN: But what were you asking?

STEFAN: Your surname.

MARTIN: Yes. Reinhardt. But not my name in this.

STEFAN: Jewish?

MARTIN: You can fictionalise it, anything you like, but not my name.

STEFAN: Okay, so what do I call you?

MARTIN: Stefan.

STEFAN: Your name is?

MARTIN: Martin, but you call me Stefan.

STEFAN: Yes.

MARTIN: Which is your name, no?

STEFAN: Yes, but then –

MARTIN: Confusing?

STEFAN: – they will think I am the one who has the story –

MARTIN: So call me Ludwig.

STEFAN: Ludwig? Too old. Ludwig van Beethoven. Ah?

MARTIN: Er, Wolfgang. Wolfgang.

STEFAN: Hoffman?

MARTIN: Amadeus Mozart –

STEFAN: No, I know a Wolfgang.

MARTIN: Johann. Kurt, Fritz, Sven. Sven.

STEFAN: Sven. Okay, Sven. I write Sven –

MARTIN: Sven Hassel.

STEFAN: Sven, Sven.

MARTIN: He wrote all the Nazi books –

STEFAN: No, Sven Hassel, we can't call it Sven Hassel –

MARTIN: Just Sven, not the Hassel. Sven –

STEFAN: Sven what? Geissmar?

MARTIN: Sven… Who's he? Gazman.

STEFAN: Sven Gazman?

MARTIN: Gazman. Gazman's a clothing chain, but it's good enough.

STEFAN: Sven Deichmann.

MARTIN: Sven Gazman. Who's Deichmann?

STEFAN: A shoe store. Sven Deichmann.

MARTIN: It's too well-known.

STEFAN: That's why it's good. Okay, Sven Diceman.

MARTIN: Gazman.

STEFAN: Gicemar.

MARTIN: Gazman.

STEFAN: Gazman. How do you spell it?

MARTIN: G-A-Z-M-A-N.

STEFAN: That's not a German name.

 MARTIN: What is it?

STEFAN: It's a made-up, stupid – guy who runs a petrol station in America.

MARTIN: Gasman. This is Gaz. G-A-Z.

STEFAN: Yes but that's how they spell Gaz in America.

MARTIN: Ooooff!

STEFAN: All right. So I come up with a name which is not your name Martin, all right?

MARTIN: Yes.

STEFAN: So you are not Martin, right?

MARTIN: No, I'm not, I am Martin, but we call me what? Sven.

STEFAN: Yeah yeah yeah yeah.

Pause.

MARTIN: So I told you about the seven hours, watched this guy bleed to death, in my condominium, until the police arrived. Took him away. I had to pay them to take him away, you know?

Pause.

Why are you looking like that at me?

STEFAN: Sorry, I was distracted.

MARTIN: By?

STEFAN: The idea of somebody bleeding in your flat to death.

MARTIN: Yes. Not nice. Anyway, so I met him there. Oam, his name was.

STEFAN: Yes.

MARTIN: Oam.

STEFAN: Like a unit of electric.

MARTIN: O A M.

STEFAN: Ah, not like a unit of electric.

MARTIN: I went out with him, I came back, I went out to sell ecstasy, I came back, he'd slit his wrists, lying there on the carpet bleeding to death for seven hours.

STEFAN: So he's depressed, yeah?

MARTIN: Why do you say that?

STEFAN: Well why he slash his wrists?

MARTIN: Wanted attention. Didn't I tell you this yesterday?

STEFAN: Oh yeah yeah yeah, you were saying, yeah.

MARTIN: Or was that somebody else I was telling you about?

STEFAN: Same guy?

MARTIN: I mean – forget it. Forget it.

STEFAN: The same guy wanted to throw himself off the balcony?

MARTIN: (*Pointing at scar.*) Same guy did this.

STEFAN: See this one here? The line here? It's where a bullet skimmed across in Sarajevo.

MARTIN: Sarajevo?

STEFAN: Yes, I was there in my twenties.

MARTIN: Lucky to be here then, no?

STEFAN: Yeah, I guess it was my reaction, I just sensed something and I tilted my head back.

MARTIN: I've got one too, from the boy in the house opposite in East Germany.

STEFAN: I've got one here too from the old times…and you see this one here…and here also.

MARTIN: Yes, enough, okay.

STEFAN: And you know what that is? It's where Ulrike Schneider broke my heart. Hahahahahaha.

MARTIN: Anyway.

STEFAN: *Jaws.* So tell from the top, from the start.

MARTIN: Well, first there was Oat, a sissy Chinese guy from Krabi. He moved in with me, all going very well until one day he said to me 'I want to be your boss.' I said 'Huh?' He said 'Yes, I want you to be my good boy.' I said oh, okay, yes, you know, because I'm open-minded, in sex and everything, and so it was fine, being his good boy for a few weeks and then one morning he said 'Okay, today you transfer half a million Baht to my bank account.' I said no, not your good boy any more. We had a fight there on the escalator in MBK. He tried to push me over the side. And as I was going out of the building my eyes met this guy going up the escalator on the other side. Oam. A kind of queeny, bitchy, tanned skin guy from the North East. But nice family, seemed honest. Of course I didn't know Bangkok then, didn't know you can't trust anyone. So I gave him a home. Looked after him, paid for his university fees, international school, everything. One day I come back, the condominium's empty. Of course it's him. He comes home, I forgive him, we buy all the things again, big drama, lots of crisis, drama queen, this kind of thing, next day tries to throw himself off the balcony. Pull him back by his foot, you stupid boy bah bah bah bah bah – take him to hospital, get psychiatrist for him, everything, all organised, give him lots of money, ten thousand a day, and then he cuts me. Slashes me. Here, you see. I had to have seven stitches here on my cheek.

STEFAN: With what?

MARTIN: Broken bottle.

STEFAN: No.

MARTIN: Heineken.

STEFAN: Really.

MARTIN: Then, few months later –

STEFAN: I must make a note of that. I had only four in this one – (*Pointing at his faint eye scar.*)

MARTIN: – came back, having sold pills in Suan Lum night bazaar, came back, he was lying there, bleeding all over the carpet.

STEFAN: Again with the bottle?

MARTIN: Yes. I mean I'm worried. I have two hundred yaa baa in the bathroom, thirty ecstasy pills under the sofa. Police come and see body lying there, what do I do?

STEFAN: Where do you get your ecstasy pills? Where do you get?

MARTIN: I get from dealer in Sathorn, but can't tell you – er, remember his name.

STEFAN: Oh. And then you sell them here to…?

MARTIN: I buy them cheap and sell them to foreigners mostly.

STEFAN: Foreigners looking for parties?

MARTIN: Mmm.

STEFAN: Flaglang?

MARTIN: Hmm?

STEFAN: Farang? Flaglang? Faglan?

MARTIN: Farang.

STEFAN: Yah, Flang looking for parties. So is it good stuff?

MARTIN: Mmm?

STEFAN: Is it good MDMA?

MARTIN: Yeah, it's good.

STEFAN: Have you tried liquid MDMA?

MARTIN: No. You?

STEFAN: Yeah, in Tehran.

MARTIN: In Tehran?

STEFAN: Yes.

MARTIN: Good?

STEFAN: It's the best stuff.

MARTIN: How long does it last? The high.

STEFAN: Thirty-six hours.

MARTIN: Oh I must try that.

STEFAN: Yes.

MARTIN: Mmm. No, it's good, it's good stuff. Sometimes we have um er what do you call kit, er – ketamine. They give it to knock out horses and things, it's good.

Pause.

STEFAN: Were you on that that night?

MARTIN: I don't want to tell you that now. Okay? I want to see what you make of this. You going to write it up?

STEFAN: Yes. You wanna read it? Before I finish?

MARTIN: Or you read it to me.

STEFAN: Yeah, I can write it and I can read it out to you.

As STEFAN reaches for his notebook he is distracted by his newspaper, which he begins to read.

MARTIN notices a badge on STEFAN's book.

MARTIN: Is that Che Guevara? Smiling? Or someone else?

STEFAN: It's an attempt to give myself an identity.

MARTIN: Oh. What you read?

STEFAN: Stars.

MARTIN: Can I see?

Pause.

STEFAN: No. My tarot cards say that they think that they will stay that way unless I change something which the cards don't specify.

MARTIN: You know, I can read. I can read the tarot. Do you want me to read you? You want a reading?

STEFAN: No, we're writing your story.

MARTIN: But I can give you a reading now. It relates to another story. Okay? Okay?

STEFAN: Yes.

MARTIN: A story about a horoscope.

STEFAN: Yeah, sure.

MARTIN: You're sure you're ready for this? Another one? It's not information overload?

STEFAN: No, I'm ready.

MARTIN: OK. So, I had a girlfriend – er, ladyboy friend. And she…he into astrology, no? Big thing here in Bangkok. She said she wants it read, wants to get a reading. So we're walking down the street in Silom one day and we see a guy sitting there on a blanket spread out like this, people queuing up to see him, so we queue up. And he does the cards, all this bollocks, and she's there going 'Mm, mm, mm', like this, and he's going 'Blah blah blah blah' like this, and when it's all finished I say to her 'So, what did he say to you?' She said 'Ah, he said I'm going to have a new love when I'm twenty-nine.' I said 'Twenty-nine? That's next month.' She said 'Yes.' I said 'Okay, so maybe I leave you now then.' She said 'Not like that, no. Not like that!' I said 'What you mean? Why your eyes light up when you tell me you're going to have new love when you're twenty-nine? Excited at this prospect, huh? Maybe I leave you now, then. You sit there, wait for this new love in your life.'

STEFAN laughs.

You think it funny? I don't think it funny. Anyway, I left her. Now she's twenty-nine and she's got no new lover.

STEFAN: You're a bit of a cunt, Martin.

MARTIN: Don't call me a cunt, Stefan. You believe in this bollax? I said to her life isn't decided by some man sitting cross-legged on the street, is it? You can decide your own life. Not directed by some guy sitting on the street on some blanket, no? What you think?

STEFAN: That's not what they say in Liberia, you know.

MARTIN: Yes, but it's Buddhism…stupid.

STEFAN: Huh?

MARTIN: It's stupid thing.

STEFAN: It's everything, everyone, everywhere.

MARTIN: You believe it too?

STEFAN: Everyone needs hope, you know? This is what religion sells. I got this friend of mine in Liberia, he has er intestinal cancer of some sort.

MARTIN: Really, where's that?

STEFAN: Liberia? West Africa.

MARTIN: Never heard of it.

STEFAN: Ha!

MARTIN: You've made it up.

STEFAN: You've never heard of Liberia? You've heard of Sierra Leone, Burkina Faso.

MARTIN: Yes.

STEFAN: It's in there, okay.

MARTIN: You been there too?

STEFAN: Chad? You heard of Chad?

MARTIN: I know a boy called Chad.

STEFAN: Anyway my friend in Liberia with the cancer he goes to this witch doctor who pretends to make a hole in your body and pulls out like the poisoned thing, but it's just chicken bits, it's not the cancer, and hey presto it comes back again. You know, Sai Baba does the same. He manifests vibhuti from thin air, and then fiddles with little boys and hands the parents a Rolex watch as payment. He's probably got the most sucked cock in the whole of the southern hemisphere.

MARTIN: This is too much.

STEFAN: What, too much information? I fucking hate this phrase. How can you, you know, know too much?

MARTIN: You can, sometimes people tell you too much.

STEFAN: No, it's because you can't deal with it, you don't want to deal with it because you're a selfish fucker who just wants to get on with his next McDonald's meal.

MARTIN: Anyway, you want to hear the stories?

STEFAN: Which reminds me, you can get a McDonald's in Liberia.

MARTIN: Get one here in Bangkok.

STEFAN: They said to me… 'How do you cope, you know, with all this suffering? All these dead bodies in the refugee camps?' You just take one day to yourself, you put on a tweed suit, go to a five star restaurant –

MARTIN: And you did that?

STEFAN: No, because I didn't have a tweed suit. And I thought where the fuck do I find a five star restaurant in a refugee camp?

MARTIN: Just make it, make it in your tent, make it up.

STEFAN: So yes, we went to the capital, Princetown, and there was a McDonald's and this was the idea of luxury – most locals can't afford it, except those with the corrupt drug money, the oil money, the blood diamond money.

MARTIN: Sounds good.

STEFAN: *Blood Diamond*, it's all about this.

MARTIN: Oh, Leonardo?

STEFAN: Sierra Leone.

MARTIN: Oi! But last night…last night I was talking to this boy, last night, called – actually, you know, he was called Boy. And I was saying to him that he looked very good when he dressed up as a lady. He said when he entered competitions for ladyboys he always won. Tell me the next time, I said, I'll come and support you, and he was telling me that in the country these Asians –

STEFAN: Are they good? The ladyboys?

MARTIN: Uuee, no. Bad. Thai actors the same. It's like – in a ladyboy show, all the emotions are done big. It's all 'Oh!' This kind of thing.

STEFAN: Do they actually have lines? Or everybody just miming pop songs?

MARTIN: They have some woman who is ladyboy, central one, usually a bit grotesque.

STEFAN: Making filthy things?

MARTIN: Talks to the audience.

STEFAN: Filthy?

MARTIN: Mmmm, not really.

STEFAN: So not saying like (*Singing.*) '– Like a Virgin fucked for the very first time– ' or 'I'm your penis, I'm your fire, your desire.'

MARTIN: No. Not like that, no.

STEFAN: Nothing like that.

MARTIN: No. But talks to the audience. 'Where are you from?' 'Have you got a wife?' In this horrible voice, like that.

STEFAN: Flirting with the audience.

MARTIN: 'Yeah…' In this horrible voice.

STEFAN: Ah, and? Then what happens?

MARTIN: They do – a bit – lip-synching bollax and –

STEFAN: Song and dance.

MARTIN: Stupid dances.

STEFAN: Yeah.

MARTIN: That kind of stuff.

STEFAN: Do they show their genitals?

MARTIN: Not my cup of tea at all. Huh? No. No, not like that.

STEFAN: So it's just guys in dresses, like a drag show, but much better.

MARTIN: Yes. Some of the women look very good. Some of the ladyboys look actually better than real women.

STEFAN: And this is why you go to see this show.

MARTIN: Me? I don't go.

STEFAN: Then how do you know so much?

MARTIN: I've seen, by mistake, by accident, I don't go.

STEFAN: You invest money, you go to the ladyboy show, you like it.

MARTIN: I've been in clubs and suddenly, you want to see the disco, but they have a stupid show on first.

STEFAN: Yeah, by accident.

MARTIN: Finish the show and let's get on with the dancing.

STEFAN: By accident you paid 2500 Bahts.

MARTIN: Don't pay.

STEFAN: To go and see a ladyboy show.

MARTIN: No, you don't pay usually, no.

STEFAN: Because you wanted to see something after it.

MARTIN: Oh shut up.

STEFAN: But you were early and you were –

MARTIN: Yes yes yes, yes, yes, you know the answer, of course.

STEFAN: Watching by mistake.

MARTIN: Oh. Anyway, the point is, we were talking about – we were talking about these – ah, I know what I wanted to tell you about. In the country these Asians they roll wet frogs in talcum powder, wait for powder to dry and then look on the skin for numbers to win the lottery. You switch on TV –

STEFAN: Why you say this about all Asians are this, all Asians are that?

MARTIN: Didn't say –

STEFAN: All Asians are –

MARTIN: I didn't say, you're putting words in my mouth.

STEFAN: Ah no, you say all Asians are lazy, all Asians are –

MARTIN: I didn't say that!

STEFAN: – are naïve.

MARTIN: You're saying it. Not me.

STEFAN: Naïve, what else?

MARTIN: I didn't say that.

STEFAN: Denial is the first step to repetition.

MARTIN: You're drawing –

STEFAN: You are maybe one step away from genocide.

MARTIN: Oh.

STEFAN: You are stage four –

MARTIN: Bollax.

STEFAN: Stage four genocide.

MARTIN: Okay, tell me the stages then. Come on.

STEFAN: Stage one.

MARTIN: What?

STEFAN: You classify them. Two: you symbolise them. Three: you dehumanise them.

MARTIN: Okay, let's look at you.

STEFAN: Four: you organise them. Yourself. Five: you polarise yourselves, from them. Six: you prepare. Seven: you exterminate. Eight: you deny it. And you are already denying, so you have done number eight, one, two, three, four, and probably five, you just haven't done six and seven, so I should just bring you a machete from China and let you get on with it.

MARTIN: Okay, go and get it, then.

STEFAN: And you don't want to cut off someone's head just for the fun. 'Cos ultimately you say you like this place, but you think they're just a bunch of yellow –

MARTIN: Yes, anyway –

STEFAN: Yellow shit.

MARTIN: Yes, but you seen the TV here? You switch it on and there's always some cute girl who the audience are clapping because she looks like she's nineteen when in fact she is fifty-six, or there's some married couple and the husband's only just discovered after one year that his wife's a ladyboy and he doesn't mind at all – more audience clapping…oooh.

STEFAN: *Constant Gardener.*

MARTIN: Huh?

STEFAN: I think something interesting is happening for you. Meaning you should not be in Thailand.

MARTIN: Where should I be?

STEFAN: You should be back in Germany.

MARTIN: Doing what?

STEFAN: Doing lawyer work. And you should be there very soon otherwise you will die here. If you want you can take your Thai back with you, one or two, import them –

MARTIN: My what?

STEFAN: Your Thai people.

MARTIN: Oh.

STEFAN: Whoever you want to fuck.

MARTIN: Yes.

STEFAN: Take them back like as a present to yourself, but you must get out of here.

MARTIN: Why?

STEFAN: Because otherwise you will die here, within five years. Yes. That is what it means.

Pause.

Do you always bathe with your clothes on?

MARTIN: Not fully clothed, no, not like these Asians, you see them doing that.

STEFAN: I feel a bit shy you know walking round naked – seems odd, but most Germans don't seem to have a problem with it.

MARTIN: Different?

STEFAN: Yah, most Germans are not self conscious at all.

MARTIN: No I don't mind. Just like, like, no.

STEFAN: You know I once saw a man in one of these inland seas in the old coal, open faced coal...open cast coal mining...and it's now a beautiful inland sea, very hot day. There's this man, skin head, swastika tattoos very, very neo Nazi looking, red face big beer belly drinking a can of, a huge can of beer, naked, totally naked on a busy beach.

MARTIN: Mm.

STEFAN: Well, on a busy edge of a lake standing ankle deep in the water, drinking this can of lager talking to somebody and he just starts pissing.

MARTIN: I knew you were going to say that.

STEFAN: Just starts pissing openly.

MARTIN: This true?

STEFAN: Openly pissing, doesn't even touch his cock, you know, he's just pouring it in one end and pissing it out the other.

MARTIN: Like a horse.

STEFAN: Kospudener Sea it was called. Kospudener Sea.

MARTIN: It was called.

STEFAN: That was the name of the lake.

Pause.

MARTIN: A-a-a-a-a... You know...normally I was supposed to become criminal, early stages of childhood, but erm – or gangster or whatever. And I was always concerned how I would turn out in relation to my own background. I mean you are hit, you become a hitter, you are raped you become a raper. But I never...and army time...very, very tough time, very bad time, nice time. But accidentally I survived. And after that I went to Berlin to continue my gay studies – er, law studies – and there I got in touch for the first time with the with gay scene... I saw discotheque where guys danced together – hug and kissed – was – ah – quite new for me. You must know, communist country don't have porn magazine, don't have porn videos, don't have any kind of gay stuff, don't have. And for quite long time being gay was also er prohibited… So I enjoy a lot, because I was twenty-two, looked like eighteen, at seventeen need to show my ID card everywhere because I looked so young, and all the guys came to me and invite me for drinks and this and that and I thought this could be my new family, thought they really liked me, but no, they only wanted to fuck me.

STEFAN: So now you are a coldhearted lover because you opened yourself up and were hurt?

MARTIN: Yes, I am too open always to girlfriend or boyfriend.

STEFAN: Which is why you had…all the possessions stolen from the flat.

MARTIN: Yes, that was the same boy did that.

STEFAN: Where has he put all this stuff?

MARTIN: Sold everything.

STEFAN: All? Drugs?

MARTIN: Money.

STEFAN: Drugs?

MARTIN: No, just money.

STEFAN: So?

MARTIN: He had no job you see. Lazy, like the rest of them. But not as bad as Pure. He was so lazy he would just wake up in the morning feeling horny and want to fuck me. Then lie down again. That's it. Went on for weeks like this.

STEFAN: So you like to receive?

MARTIN: Yes, so in the end I said to him come on, there must be one thing that interests you. Just one thing. So he thought for very long time and then he said 'Skateboard'. I said fine, okay, we take you to Carrefour on Rama 4 and get you a skateboard. We got there, he said this one's fine. I said wait a minute, maybe there's cheaper one, better model in Tesco Lotus over the road. He said no, this one's fine. You know why he said that? Too fucking lazy to cross the road to Tesco Lotus.

STEFAN: So drama queen?

MARTIN: Me?

STEFAN: No, he say – you say he's a – he said –

MARTIN: He said I called him drama queen. I never said that.

STEFAN: Because he's so emotional?

MARTIN: Yeah, and attempts for attention and all this stuff.

STEFAN: Begging you to take him back.

MARTIN: Anyway. Dead now.

STEFAN: So then he slashed his wrists and you didn't try to bind them up and stop the bleeding?

MARTIN: No.

STEFAN: He blacked out in the flat?

MARTIN: Well when I came back from selling ecstasy he was half – half dead already.

STEFAN: He was dead.

MARTIN: Lying in a pool of his own blood. No, still alive. Still breathing. I thought what do I do? So I sit, I wait, I watch him. I just sit in a chair and watch. Watch him bleeding.

STEFAN: So why didn't you help him? Are you like hungover or are you –

MARTIN: No, just, just – I don't know.

STEFAN: Tired?

MARTIN: Weird.

STEFAN: Tired?

MARTIN: Weird.

STEFAN: Tired.

MARTIN: No.

STEFAN: Not tired.

MARTIN: Just feeling weird.

STEFAN: Weird, yeah. So when the police came how could you talk to them?

MARTIN: I didn't need to say very much. At that time I don't speak much Thai, and their English not good.

STEFAN: Yeah.

MARTIN: The situation speaks for itself.

STEFAN: Which was he's dead in a pool of blood from what?

MARTIN: Looked like.

STEFAN: You stabbed him?

MARTIN: He killed himself.

STEFAN: The police? What they say to you?

MARTIN: I paid them…

STEFAN: How much? Lots?

MARTIN: A hundred thousand.

STEFAN: Bats?

MARTIN: Mm?

STEFAN: Bats?

MARTIN: Yes.

STEFAN: How much is it in Deutschmark? Or Euro.

MARTIN: It's about a hundred and fifty Euro. One thousand five hundred Euro.

STEFAN: Yah, so not so bad.

MARTIN: But it's a lot to them.

STEFAN: Yah, like several months' wages.

MARTIN: A year.

STEFAN: A year's salary. And they take the body away and end of story. The credits roll, Martin lays a wreath and pours milk at the shrine, camera pans out, we see other mourners also laying other wreaths and pouring other milk at other shrines, we go up into the sky there are thousands of mourners, thousands of shrines, pouring thousands of milks – maybe some of the actors who have been playing the parts walk up to the shrines with the survivors, lay a few wreaths on the shrines of those who did not survive… What about the Oam's family?

MARTIN: Fortunately he had no relatives.

STEFAN: Nothing? Anything? Brothers? Sisters?

MARTIN: An orphan.

STEFAN: So he just he's dead? Where is he buried? In the temple for people without relatives?

MARTIN: I told you, yes.

STEFAN: So when do you pray?

MARTIN: I paid for his coffin. I paid five hundred Baht.

STEFAN: And his body is there? In this place?

MARTIN: Been burned now.

STEFAN: Cremated.

MARTIN: Mmm.

STEFAN: End of story.

MARTIN: End of Oam.

STEFAN: End of Oam, end of story. If it's going to end like that it is to have more possibility. For my taste, anyway – like *Broken Flowers* or *Spiderman Two*.

MARTIN: Maybe.

STEFAN: Well, what else happens?

MARTIN: Other stories?

STEFAN: Maybe? Yeah tell me other stories.

MARTIN: No, you tell me. Tell me something about yourself.

STEFAN: I'm thirty-six, I have a wife, I have –

MARTIN: Wife?

STEFAN: Yes, what about her?

MARTIN: So you like pussy.

STEFAN: I have balls, they need emptying.

MARTIN: So come on, read me something you've written.

STEFAN: But I haven't heard a story yet.

MARTIN: Okay, Berlin, law studies blah blah blah, er then became money-boy. Just put up advertisement saying blonde, thirty, good-looking, will do anything. And after two weeks the phone wouldn't stop ringing. But it was all old, ugly guys.

STEFAN: What sort of thing they ask you?

MARTIN: Just wanted companionship, most of them, I sit there, watch TV, make me sandwich, this kind of thing.

STEFAN: Okay, boring, so what was the worst thing you had to do?

MARTIN: Oh, caca in the mouth.

STEFAN: Yeah?

MARTIN: Yes, this guy…no, no, I said, I can't do that, no, draw the line, but this guy very insistent, please, please do it in my mouth, I said not in the mouth, no, too much, he said please, I said okay I can do it at home and bring it to you, feed you, with a spoon, he said no, has to be from the arse – warm and fresh, I said okay, I bring it and we heat it up in the microwave. Jing jing.

Pause.

So I told you I got the scar, yeah?

STEFAN: Yeah, but you didn't tell me why the scar, and when the scar.

MARTIN: Did I tell you about Bum?

STEFAN: No, tell me –

MARTIN: Or what was his name? Shit, no. Shit. Or was it, was it…Wit? I can't remember now.

STEFAN: What, somebody's nickname, or –

MARTIN: They've all got names like Wit, Shit, Bum, Coco, Whisky, Tan, Tit –

STEFAN: Yeah.

MARTIN: Fuck, Fuck-wit – maybe that was it.

STEFAN: Okay, so yeah –

MARTIN: So Fuck-wit. His name was Fuck-wit, okay? He stole the computer off my back.

STEFAN: How did he do that?

MARTIN: Went to this place, a backpack with my new G4 in, I said could you look after it for me, turned round five minutes later it had gone.

STEFAN: So you just gave it to him ?

MARTIN: Everything. Just to look after.

STEFAN: You know this guy?

MARTIN: Yeah, I met him the night before, but he won't show up now you won't see him for a few months, you know? But this is all background. More important stories than this, okay?

STEFAN: Yes.

MARTIN: It's not about this.

STEFAN: But he was a prostitute?

MARTIN: That's going a bit far, no?

STEFAN: Why? Somebody takes money for sex, you call them a prostitute.

MARTIN: Okay, so I'm a prostitute, yes? You are a prostitute in some way.

STEFAN: No, I'm not a prostitute –

MARTIN: In a manner of speaking we're all prostitutes here, we all take money for something, no? Don't start getting moralistic on me, okay?

STEFAN: I'm not getting moralistic. I'm just trying to clarify what is money-boy as opposed to prostitute, there's no difference. So this boy in the flat, was he a money-boy?

MARTIN: No.

STEFAN: So how do you know he was not a money-boy?

MARTIN: Some of them are very subtle.

STEFAN: So you never know?

MARTIN: No, some of them you know, some of them –

STEFAN: So when do you give them the money? Never?

MARTIN: Some of them maybe you don't give money, you just spend money on them.

STEFAN: Oh like drinks, percentage.

MARTIN: Maybe. Take them to dinner, buy them some clothes, this kind of thing.

STEFAN: Yeah. And they ask you for this?

MARTIN: Mmmm, not directly. But it's expected.

STEFAN: Implied.

MARTIN: Mmm.

STEFAN: So you have to go and buy some –

MARTIN: Oh you take them to dinner, expensive restaurant, at the end of the meal they go 'Checkbin krub!' And the checkbin comes and they go…

He slides an imaginary bill towards STEFAN.

STEFAN: They slide to you so you have to pay.

MARTIN: Mmm.

STEFAN: It's expensive, no…

MARTIN: Not for me, no. Not for us from the West.

STEFAN: Yah, okay so he's not a money-boy. Who was he? A friend? Someone you know?

MARTIN: Someone I got to know. I just met him in DJ, and er became friendly. Mmm.

STEFAN: So he's a con artist? Scam?

MARTIN: I would say he's a drama queen, more than a con artist.

STEFAN: Another drama queen?

MARTIN: Not a money-boy, no.

STEFAN: But now he's dead, yeah?

MARTIN: Yes.

STEFAN: And you killed him.

MARTIN: Oi!

STEFAN: So how did he die?

MARTIN: I told you that, no?

STEFAN: No, you didn't say –

MARTIN: That was the same one, Oam – Oam on the floor, he did that.

STEFAN: So what? With the Heineken bottle?

MARTIN: Yes, that was Oam.

STEFAN: Oh for fuck's sake.

Pause.

MARTIN: Are you okay? (*He hands STEFAN a pill.*) You want one of these? I have to keep them by my balls. Sorry. Smelly?

STEFAN: Smells of your balls.

MARTIN: Yes, sweaty. I should put them in tissue. Stop them drying out.

STEFAN: What? Really?

MARTIN: Mmm.

STEFAN: You keep them by your balls so they don't dry out?

MARTIN: No, in tissue so they don't dry out. I mean so they don't get wet. Sorry, moisture.

STEFAN: From your balls?

MARTIN: Or any moisture, in the air –

STEFAN: Yeah, but your balls are sweating, the tissue's going soft with the sweat –

MARTIN: Yes, but I put them in the tissue to try and keep them dry, away from the tissue, the balls and the sweat.

STEFAN: Why don't you put them in –

MARTIN: My arse?

STEFAN: No, in the tin foil, or something?

MARTIN: It hurts, by the…tin foil by the balls hurts.

STEFAN: Well, cling-film then.

MARTIN: What's wrong with tissue?

STEFAN: Because it absorbs the sweats from your balls, and then – then the sweat –

MARTIN: Not if you wrap it up about three times, the sweat can't get through.

STEFAN: How sweaty are your balls?

MARTIN: Depends, doesn't it, on the situation.

STEFAN: Well, in this climate my balls are sweating all the time.

MARTIN: If I'm in a car and there are six policemen surrounding it then I'm sweating a lot, I tell you.

STEFAN: Yeah, so then the sweat goes through the tissue papers and into the pills –

MARTIN: Look, this is not the story I want, it's not – I don't – these stories about drug stories, no drug stories, no money-boy stories. Something else, okay?

STEFAN: Okay, no money-boys, no drugs, no –

MARTIN: There's more important stories than this. There's stories about people dying, mass murder, things like this. Stuff that's not funny. No?

STEFAN: I'm not laughing.

MARTIN: Not funny. That's the stuff that doesn't make me laugh. Mass murder, you know?

STEFAN: Okay so go back to the mass murder – the mist rises…there's a boy sleeping on your shoulder…and there in front of you, you see a pile of bodies, higher than the buildings. Or you're driving along the road and it's dark, and lumpy lumpy lumpy lumpy lumpy, and then, oh the road's lumpy today. The sun comes up, you realise you're driving over bodies. You're driving along the street, and there's logs piled up at the side. At least that's what you think. It's actually bodies. Er you dive in a pile of bodies and hide. You get…you're walking to the big place where the slaughter was and under your feet crack crack crack crack crack. You look down, you're walking on skulls. What's your best genocide moment?

MARTIN: Don't have one.

STEFAN: You been to Auschwitz?

MARTIN: I've been to Auschwitz.

STEFAN: Been to Dachau?

MARTIN: Been to Dachau.

STEFAN: Been to Belsen?

MARTIN: Belsen.

STEFAN: Been to the Killing Fields?

MARTIN: Been.

STEFAN: You like it?

MARTIN: No.

STEFAN: So why you go?

MARTIN: Well, it's a long story, begins with the pigs on my grandparents' farm.

STEFAN: So start at the beginning.

MARTIN: I was born in a small town, not far from Polish border. 30,000 citizen only. My mother was a child of the war. Until I was fourteen I worked on my grandparents' farm. Everything about agriculture I know.

STEFAN: And when did you first realise you like catamite fun?

MARTIN: Cata what? What you mean?

STEFAN: You know…sodomy.

MARTIN: Gay?

STEFAN: Mmm.

MARTIN: Well, I'm not gay at all.

STEFAN: Do you meet some farmhand? Involving animals? Sheep, pigs?

MARTIN: Nothing like that. I also worked recycling rubbish, glasses and bottles, this kind of thing. And the money, had to give all to my mother – and she never gave back. Years went on like this.

STEFAN: I had a cat once lick my cock. You know when I was first discovering –

MARTIN: A cat?

STEFAN: Erections.

MARTIN: Yeugh.

STEFAN: No, it's nice, abrasive…very good for hot teenage cock.

MARTIN: No, wouldn't like that.

STEFAN: They must like the salty flavour. Especially the hot teenage salty flavour.

MARTIN: Yeugh, yuch.

STEFAN: You know the –

MARTIN: I don't want to think about that.

STEFAN: Leakages.

MARTIN: I don't like animals at all.

STEFAN: Mm.

MARTIN: Yurrch.

STEFAN: So you never put your finger in a girl's…you know…

MARTIN: What?

STEFAN: Hair band.

MARTIN: Hair band?

STEFAN: Yeah, you've got the hair band round the ponytail and if you put your finger through the hair inside the hair band, it feels like you're going in and out of an arsehole.

MARTIN: Really?

STEFAN: Yes, it's interesting.

MARTIN: The thing for tying up the ponytail?

STEFAN: They call them bungees or something…scrunches.

MARTIN: An arsehole?

STEFAN: Yeah, if you put your finger in the middle of the hair and you get this sort of tension and release and it's like you're pressing in somebody's arsehole. I always ask my girlfriends if I can do it if they are wearing a ponytail.

MARTIN: Why don't you do the real thing?

STEFAN: I dunno, it's just more fun you know to put your finger in someone's hair and get the idea of it. I mean you can't penetrate an arsehole in the high street but you can put your finger in someone's hair band anywhere...on the metro. If you've got a willing friend.

MARTIN: I guess so.

STEFAN: A lot of my fag-hag friends let me...they think it's great...

MARTIN: Oh, I don't like the way this conversation is going. I don't like. So ugly, these words, all these words, cock and...and...yeugh. Sick. I'm beginning to feel sick.

STEFAN: What's your problem with talking biologically?

MARTIN: Huh?

STEFAN: If I talked about pulling out the intestines and so forth –

MARTIN: Don't want to hear about it.

STEFAN: The cock is a piece of a body.

MARTIN: Let's talk about the weather or something like that.

STEFAN: Okay, so...

MARTIN: Yes, it's nice, huh?

STEFAN: No, I think it's quite humid.

MARTIN: Hmm, as usual.

STEFAN: So why you like it here? Because you say you fell in love with Thailand, but obviously it's not because of the weather.

MARTIN: No, the people – I told you – the people are very sweet and nice –

STEFAN: All of them –

MARTIN: Most of them are. Of course you get horrible people, but – like everywhere – people are nice, and it reminds me –

STEFAN: So is there anything to see here?

MARTIN: Huh? You mean tourist?

STEFAN: Yes. You done those things?

MARTIN: Yes I've been to Jim Thompson's house, you know? The guy, the silk guy, you know the guy who disappeared.

STEFAN: Interesting?

MARTIN: You know this guy? American who disappeared then left this big house behind.

STEFAN: For the public.

MARTIN: Silk, he made silk. He disappeared, never found him.

STEFAN: When was that?

MARTIN: Mmmm, 50s.

STEFAN: So the house is now public property?

MARTIN: Yeah, it's there, you go and visit.

STEFAN: Silk is it?

MARTIN: Yeah…I've never been there actually. Just want to go to the sights, so you go to the floating market. You know the floating market? I never been there either, because I don't like doing the touristy things. You have to go there five o'clock in the morning, go there, blahblahblah, all in the little boats, all very pretty, floating market. Lots of tourists taking pictures. I've never seen. I've seen the pictures of it. It's enough.

STEFAN: To be honest Martin, I just came here for the cock.

MARTIN: Well there's plenty of that.

STEFAN: I'm married, you see.

MARTIN: Well, they'll like that, the boys will like that you know. Yeah, like the straight guys.

STEFAN: Not many straight guys here?

MARTIN: Yes there are but –

STEFAN: Why?

MARTIN: I think seventy-two per cent of men in Thailand they are bisexual.

STEFAN: You've counted them?

MARTIN: I think Thai men they don't care. If he can't have sex with his wife or any lady he don't mind, just lay there, have dick sucked by another man, as long as the man doesn't look nasty it's fine.

STEFAN: Doesn't the wife mind?

MARTIN: Yes, in Thailand it's very common.

STEFAN: What?

MARTIN: Women cutting off their husband's cock. When they find that they're unfaithful, they do it when they're asleep. It happens two or three times a week.

STEFAN: They get it reattached?

MARTIN: Don't know, I don't know about that.

STEFAN: They throw the cock away?

MARTIN: Don't know, but some guy told me yes they often put it in ice and it's sewn back on. So maybe they just do it for the humiliation, you know, and then but the wife very considerately puts it in ice. I don't know. I wouldn't want to suck it after that. Would you? Maybe it's a nice sensation, you know, like –

STEFAN: Like a lollipop.

MARTIN: Better for fucking.

STEFAN: You can just go to the supermarket and buy a frozen penis.

MARTIN: Ooof.

STEFAN: And then say it's a hot day here in Silom, it's a hot day, can I have one of those frozen penis lollies? And then you just pay your money and lick this guy's cock and slowly it gets warm. And maybe there's even a bit of seminal fluid in there for you to suck. They can perhaps attach a milk bottle, and you can suck milk.

MARTIN: Anyway –

STEFAN: But it reminds you...

MARTIN: Huh?

STEFAN: Bangkok you were saying reminds you...

MARTIN: Yes, yes, of where I grew up, of East Germany, because, you know, the slums and suburbs of Bangkok a bit like where I grew up, you know – really extreme poverty. And hardship. Very bad condition. Very tough time –

STEFAN: Let's get back to talking about the cocks, it's much more interesting –

MARTIN: No! I don't like the way – the word, I know I say it myself sometimes, but in passing, I try to rush over the word. You say 'The dog's *cock*.' I don't say the word like that. I say yes he sucked my cock and blahblahblahblahblah, but you go 'No, look at the dog's *cock*...a cat licked my *cock*.'

STEFAN: Okay, take a chill pill –

MARTIN: I don't want to dwell on it like that.

STEFAN: Okay. Tell me about your upbringing.

MARTIN: Yes, bad condition all the time.

STEFAN: Tell me all the details of the upbringing.

MARTIN: Well, it's really, really bad, lived with my mother in one room.

STEFAN: Are we talking...are we talking err –

MARTIN: She beat me every day.

STEFAN: No, wait, are we talking er *Angela's Ashes* or *A Child Called It*?

MARTIN: Never read either but I heard I think –

STEFAN: Are we talking Dave Pelzer or are we talking –

MARTIN: Don't know, don't know.

STEFAN: *Tom Sawyer*, *Huckleberry Finn*?

MARTIN: It's your job, you're the writer, I don't know.

STEFAN: What's your level?

MARTIN: Don't know, don't know.

STEFAN: No I need to know, I need to know where to get the facts from.

MARTIN: Yes, but I don't know the literature, I don't know the… I don't read. I don't understand.

STEFAN: Okay, we're on the farm, with your recycled grandmother, horny farm hands in the cold blah blah blah blah blah –

MARTIN: We lived in one room, fifth floor, me, my mother and my sister, imagine seventeen years like this, in one bed, no bathroom, just a four litre bowl, and everything…washing, washing clothes, everything you'd do in this bowl. If you wanted to go to the toilet in the night you didn't go outside in minus fifteen degrees – no, you go in the bowl, and the next day throw away. Imagine, three people like this – my mother – fat, dirty, never washed, drunk all the time, blurrhgggghhh – couldn't talk properly.

STEFAN: Not good enough.

MARTIN: And one thing she did, my mother, she hit me every day, really.

STEFAN: That's better.

MARTIN: For no reason. And if she had a reason, such as bad behaviour at school, then even more reason to hit me.

STEFAN: And then what?

MARTIN: No, I can't talk about it now… My head's full of all these boys now, these money-boy stories, bleeding on the carpet, cats licking cocks, chill pills, ecstasy by the balls. I can't take any more of it, you know?

STEFAN: So why the slashing? The slashing by the face?

MARTIN: I just wanna get high now. I go out now, okay?

STEFAN: So why can't we get high together?

MARTIN: Yeah, go and get high now, okay?

STEFAN: What's wrong with your arm?

MARTIN: Huh?

STEFAN: What's wrong with your arm?

MARTIN: No, I just – it's dancing, you know, dancing.

STEFAN: What?

MARTIN: Okay?

STEFAN: Yeah.

MARTIN: I wanna get okay, okay?

STEFAN: I wanna get dancing too.

MARTIN: See you later.

STEFAN: Yah, I'm gonna dance too.

MARTIN: Feel good, okay?

They dance. Fade to black.

Lights up.

STEFAN: So is this story is it all finished? Of the guy with the knife and the Heineken bottle?

MARTIN: I told you these aren't the interesting stories here. What's interesting is what's…this is going on underneath something else.

STEFAN: Yeah? Underneath the other thing. Something big going on in the world?

MARTIN: Could be. Could be that.

STEFAN: And you're sure it's not some sort of concocted delusion of your drug-riddled mind?

MARTIN: It's not drug-riddled. How could I be a practising lawyer and have a drug-riddled mind?

STEFAN: 'Cos you can take lots of drugs, I have a friend who is injecting speed and he is a very good engineer. He's held his job down for years, he's on –

MARTIN: What's his name?

STEFAN: His name? Clive.

MARTIN: Oh. Don't know him.

STEFAN: He's injecting speed in his eyeballs.

MARTIN: Really?

STEFAN: And he still manages –

MARTIN: Dangerous.

STEFAN: Yeah, but it's good, he likes it, it's a good drug, he's made lots of friends –

MARTIN: No, it's bad, bad drug.

STEFAN: No, he's made lots of friends. It works for him because he's very lethargic.

MARTIN: I take speed, but not – smoke speed sometimes.

STEFAN: Maybe your personality is wrong.

MARTIN: I'm already speedy, that's the problem.

STEFAN: Yah, see with Clive he is very lethargic and the speed brings him up. He's er forty-six.

MARTIN: No bad effect on his health?

STEFAN: No, not apparently. We play basketball together.

MARTIN: Really?

STEFAN: He always beats me.

MARTIN: You play basketball?

STEFAN: Fifty nil usually.

MARTIN: That's 'cos he's on speed.

STEFAN: Maybe I should take some too and then [I could beat him] –

MARTIN: I'm very good at bowling when I'm on speed.

STEFAN: Ten-pin bowling?

MARTIN: Yes, when I'm on speed it's much better.

STEFAN: Ten-pin bowling is a game for idiots.

MARTIN: I score strikes all the time when I'm on speed.

STEFAN: Dim-wit idiots.

MARTIN: Yes, like me.

STEFAN: Means nothing, it's just chuck a ball down the fucking alleyway and –

MARTIN: I know, I know. I like it.

STEFAN: So tell me your story.

MARTIN: Well funnily enough it started in bowling.

STEFAN: Yeah.

MARTIN: I was playing bowling with a few guys –

STEFAN: Yeah.

MARTIN: And a girl, and I had a new mobile phone.

STEFAN: (*Yawning.*) Yeah.

MARTIN: Are you interested in this?

STEFAN: Yeah, I think it's great.

MARTIN: You look bored.

STEFAN: No, I think, you know, it's amazing.

MARTIN: Yes? Good?

STEFAN: Bit like the *Constant Gardener*, but go on.

MARTIN: Er, it came to pay the bill, it came to pay the bill, we left, went for a drink together, went for karaoke. Went to another bar, played snooker, and we ended up on Khao San road by this stage completely fucking drunk, you know in this gay bar, called Saki, and there was this guy, this Asian guy, who wanted to fuck me in the toilet.

STEFAN: But you're not gay at all.

MARTIN: So we're in the cubicle – he's fucking me…and I had the new mobile phone in the breast pocket, here, and you know he's fucking me, like this, you know, over the bowl like this, and more and more, more like this and I could see there the phone coming more and more out, out and I was coming, no, no, the phone, and then suddenly…yes, plop! Gone.

Pause.

Two weeks later I'm having a shit –

STEFAN: Yeah.

MARTIN: In toilets in the bar in Sukhumvit 49, I looked down on the floor, there's my fucking mobile on the floor.

STEFAN: Where?

MARTIN: Two weeks later…in the toilet in the club in Sukhumvit 49.

STEFAN: So then you just took the phone?

MARTIN: There's twenty-five missed calls.

STEFAN: Yes.

MARTIN: From a guy called Martin.

STEFAN: Is it all from you?

MARTIN: And who's called Martin?

STEFAN: You.

MARTIN: Yes.

STEFAN: So you were ringing your own mobile to find yourself.

MARTIN: Yes, and then suddenly it's there.

STEFAN: So, the sim card was still in?

MARTIN: Yes.

STEFAN: And, did you notice anyone following you?

MARTIN: No.

STEFAN: So you were just being paranoid because your brain is addled with the ecstasy and –

MARTIN: Don't know what's going on. Don't know, don't know.

STEFAN: – and the heroin.

MARTIN: Don't know.

STEFAN: You think from the combination of speed, cocaine, ecstasy, ketamine, that you're arrogant and aggressive, and –

MARTIN: Possibly.

STEFAN: – you're high, and you think that you're more important than you are –

MARTIN: Maybe.

STEFAN: But in fact you're completely irrelevant little shit.

MARTIN: Maybe.

STEFAN: And nobody cares what –

MARTIN: About my stories.

STEFAN: Nothing. There's –

MARTIN: Nothing there.

STEFAN: The stories don't exist. You lost your fucking mobile, somebody found it, somebody left it somewhere else, who gives a fucking shit, everybody every day is losing the mobile, the hand palm.

MARTIN: I lose a mobile every twelve months, I lose a mobile.

STEFAN: Yeah, and I see a sign on the cashpoint –

MARTIN: I have a G4 nicked every six months –

STEFAN: Yes, so why do you buy the thing? Just like don't fucking use the things.

MARTIN: What were you going to say? You see what?

STEFAN: I see the sign on the ATM saying help – help me I have lost my palm pilot, it is my diary, my internet access –

MARTIN: On the ATM?

STEFAN: Yeah, like a photo of the –

MARTIN: Really?

STEFAN: – palm pilot, and the guy who has lost it, claiming that it is his diary, it is my internet access, it's my work, it's my diary, it's my address book, my organiser, it's my…it's my life, he says, please help. I lost it either in the city or the west end.

MARTIN: Which city?

STEFAN: In London.

MARTIN: Oh.

STEFAN: And this area is fucking huge. Where are we going to find the palm pilot in the city or the west end? So I take the sign down, because I don't give a shit and I put it in a folder at home for my fun, with my other things, like lost dogs, missing children and male rape stories on the underground.

MARTIN: You've lost your dog?

STEFAN: I haven't lost my dog. I haven't got a dog.

MARTIN: Oh come on then. You. Let's look at you. I want to know more about you.

STEFAN: What you mean?

MARTIN: This is all me, so what about you? Let's look at you.

STEFAN: Okay, young teacher, works with hard kids.

MARTIN: I thought you were in publishing.

STEFAN: I was just giving you the back story.

MARTIN: You were?

STEFAN: Yeah.

MARTIN: Okay…hurry up.

STEFAN: So you want the story? Or just the thirty second pitch?

MARTIN: Whatever.

STEFAN: Okay, young teacher, works with young kids, this is in my early twenties – hard area, lot of social problems –

MARTIN: Oh, in Berlin.

STEFAN: Yeah, in Friedrikshain. You know, the area just off Karl Marx Strasse.

MARTIN: Oh, okay.

STEFAN: Tower blocks, lots of inner city trouble, lot of rioting. And they couldn't understand them, you know, they just given up on the youth, and so I started to get them to write diaries. Journals. I paid for these journals from my own money because the school didn't even want to give them books.

MARTIN: Oh like Hilary Swank. Is it? Is that her name? The one from *Million Dollar Baby*.

STEFAN: What you say… I am *Million Dollar Baby*? This story?

MARTIN: No, no, the other one, same actress from *Million Dollar*.

STEFAN: Oh, I don't know this film, but yes I guess if you're saying which film is my story…the rubber fist is from *Borat*, the guy with the intestinal cancer guy is Jim Carey in *Man on the Moon*, all the Africa stuff was from *Blood Diamond* and *Hotel Rwanda*.

MARTIN: What? So you haven't been there?

STEFAN: No.

MARTIN: What about Tehran? You didn't take MDMA.

STEFAN: No, I just saw George Clooney do it in *Syriana*. The only thing I told that was true was the cat licking my cock.

MARTIN: I like you.

STEFAN: You don't just like Asians?

MARTIN: No, sometimes I like foreigners. But you should smile more. You look good when you smile. When you smile the whole world is beautiful.

He goes to embrace STEFAN, who pushes him off.

First time I saw you I thought this guy, interested, interesting, or interested maybe, keeps on promising going to meet me, listen to my stories, weeks go by, what's happening here? Maybe this isn't about me, this is about a guy says he wants to hear my stories but never calls me. Huh? Maybe it's about you. That's what it's about? What you think? Maybe I just give up now. Why should I give you anything? Huh?

STEFAN: Why you do this?

MARTIN: Fuck you.

STEFAN: What? Why?

MARTIN: Fuck you.

STEFAN: Why you do this?

MARTIN: Find some other foreigner to suck dry.

STEFAN: I'm not dry sucking anyone.

MARTIN: You want this story? I'll give you a fucking story!

Pause.

I was in Bangkok.

STEFAN: Yeah.

MARTIN: With this guy called Coco.

STEFAN: Yeah.

MARTIN: He said to me 'You want to take something tonight?'

STEFAN: Yeah.

MARTIN: I said okay. So we had half each. And half an hour later he said to me 'I can't feel anything.' I said 'Nor can I.' I said 'Do you want more?' So we took two more. Half an hour later I said 'I still can't feel anything.' But we noticed we were jumping up and down. He said 'Do you want to take more?' I said okay. Then we went to a straight club, in Sukhumvit Soi 11, 'cos it's open late, only place open then.

STEFAN: Sukhumvit 11?

MARTIN: Sukhumvit Soi 11. You been there?

STEFAN: No.

MARTIN: No, it's hip-hop joint, not my type of music.

STEFAN: What time is this open till?

MARTIN: Till six.

STEFAN: So you can stay dancing all night long.

MARTIN: Mmm, to hip-hop though. And er –

STEFAN: How can you dance to hip-hop?

MARTIN: Me not.

STEFAN: I suppose if you're on ecstasy you can dance to anything.

MARTIN: True, true. Then we went back to the condominium, and that's when things got funny, I think.

Pause.

And then it's black. Everything went black.

STEFAN: So you blacked out, or? When you say things went funny, what went funny?

MARTIN: He went funny. More like, remember, very vaguely he went funny. Started becoming all dramatic and intense and er telling me he loved me and that he thought we were born to be together and that he wanted to spend the rest of his life with me. A guy I'd known for a few hours… And after that I can't remember anything. But the next day I

woke up in a pool of blood. On a bathroom floor. Got up.
I didn't recognise the bathroom. I looked in the toilet and
there's a big shit floating in it. I thought what has happened
here? I've passed out on the bathroom floor, I've had a
shit, not flushed the toilet, is it my blood? Am I bleeding?
I check my body, no cuts. Maybe it came out of my mouth
in the night, I don't know. Then I ventured into the other
room. It was my room. Hadn't recognised where I was.
And another body lying on the floor in a pool of blood.
(*STEFAN is laughing.*) You find this funny?

STEFAN: No, it's sad. It's really good, really good. Nice.

MARTIN: Yes?

STEFAN: Yeah? Go on. So there's other bodies, pool of blood,
yeah.

MARTIN: Other body.

STEFAN: Yeah.

MARTIN: Lying in a pool of blood. No shit by it. Just blood.

STEFAN: Yeah. Dead?

MARTIN: Stone cold. Dead.

STEFAN: And you killed him?

MARTIN: What? What? I don't believe it. You're just like the
guy in that TV interview I saw the other night.

STEFAN: And you are Brad Pitt in *Seven*.

MARTIN: Oh fuck Brad Pitt.

STEFAN: No, you – yeah, if you want to. He's adopting some
black kids – Brangelina.

MARTIN: From Malawi? Or was that Madonna?

STEFAN: I can't remember.

MARTIN: Yeah, Malawi…no, Madonna in… Malawi in
Madonna. Madonna's in Malawi… There was a rumour
she was going to adopt a black Malawi boy.

STEFAN: What? Madonna?

MARTIN: Yes… Look, what are we talking about? Ah, you've broken my thought, my train of thought…oh God.

STEFAN: Probably, okay, rewind.

MARTIN: No, no, no…the thing. The TV interview. You know this story? Couple of backpackers in the Australian outback, some nutter killed her boyfriend, she ran away, when they found her they all thought she'd done it.

STEFAN: So it's *Wolf Creek*.

MARTIN: You see it?

STEFAN: *Wolf Creek*?

MARTIN: No, the documentary where she's interviewed on HBO.

STEFAN: Can't get it in my room.

MARTIN: Where you stay?

STEFAN: Harm Hotel.

MARTIN: Harm?

STEFAN: Used to be Charm but the C fell off.

MARTIN: Don't know. Gay?

STEFAN: It's kitsch – gay-friendly.

MARTIN: Oh , so you didn't see?

STEFAN: What?

MARTIN: The TV programme.

STEFAN: No, the only thing I watch now is the mini series *Holocaust*.

MARTIN: Oh I saw that. In the 70s.

STEFAN: It's the only thing I watch.

MARTIN: I saw it. I watched it on black and white TV in East Germany.

STEFAN: It was not on in East Germany.

MARTIN: Yes, we saw it, black and white TV. We were very privileged, we had black and white TV.

STEFAN: It was not on the East German channels.

MARTIN: We had it, with black people with their black cum, in East Germany. I saw it. Meryl Streep and James Woods.

STEFAN: See, there you go again. Black people, black cum –

MARTIN: Yes, racist, I know.

STEFAN: You are at stage six now.

MARTIN: We're all racist. Come on, everyone's racist. The Jews are racist. Oh.

STEFAN: Stage seven, you are at.

MARTIN: You're worse. You're pointing it all out.

STEFAN: I am not –

MARTIN: You are enjoying it all. Yes, you have your theory, yes, it's lovely, yes it proves my theory, great.

STEFAN: I am interested in these things, I am interested in why –

MARTIN: Oh, bollax.

STEFAN: – why you are prepared to dehumanise –

MARTIN: Why are you interested?

STEFAN: Because evil attracts me, I find it attractive, I find it interesting to see –

MARTIN: Yes, I know all that.

STEFAN: When people say yeah I see red. I think what does this mean, you see red? You get off on it, you like it, I want you to admit that. I want you to say yeah, I get off on killing people, I get off on being racist about people.

MARTIN: So you want me to kill you, is that it? You want to provoke a murder here? Yeah? Want to see some blood.

STEFAN: I don't want to see some blood.

MARTIN: Yes? Go and get the knife, then, get the weapon, I'll do it.

STEFAN: This is *The Constant Gardner*. This is it, it's the same.

MARTIN: *Constant Gardner*? You think it's good movie?

STEFAN: No. It's like *Syriana*, you know, less structure but, same kind of thing. Big portrait of the corrupt world.

MARTIN: Oh boring, boring.

STEFAN: Millions of dollars – You know, we get attached to someone, we're deliberately led astray, the image, you know, you go into hospital, you see?

MARTIN: You didn't see *Lord of War*?

STEFAN: No. Is it good?

MARTIN: That's better.

STEFAN: Is it good to see?

MARTIN: 'Cos it's more comic, more…um…

STEFAN: More fun?

MARTIN: Stylised. More fun.

STEFAN: Yes but in *Constant Gardner* –

MARTIN: And you know Nicholas Cage, he's actually –

STEFAN: If you take the image in the hospital –

MARTIN: Nicholas Cage is actually in Bangkok now, making a movie called *Bangkok Dangerous*. You know?

STEFAN: Yeah, what –

MARTIN: And I saw him on the TV, watching him with my Thai friend.

STEFAN: – what's it got to do with *Constant Gardner*?

MARTIN: Nothing, okay, but why this *Constant Gardner* all the time?

STEFAN: That's what I'm trying to tell you…you take the image in the hospital, she's pregnant, he's just been told she's been having an affair. He comes into the hospital with –

MARTIN: What affair?

STEFAN: Well, it's hinted at because they want –

MARTIN: She had an affair? I can't remember.

STEFAN: No, it's rumoured because they want to fuck the relationship up because –

MARTIN: Ah yes.

STEFAN: – she's digging – so they rumoured that the black gay guy's having an affair with her but we don't know he's gay yet. All this information is withheld from us so that when we see the image of her in the hospital looking distressed with the black baby feeding on her breasts –

MARTIN: Oh yes.

STEFAN: You think 'Ah'. The baby has come out, it's black, and he's sitting there by her. She looks distressed, the black gay guy looks distressed, the husband looks like he's on his way in to confront them…but the reason is the baby's dead and she's just letting off some milk on some other baby whose mother cannot feed it because she's dehydrated and ill. And all these stupid deceptive images while the film maker to make create the tension.

Pause.

And the music, you know, like tense music all the time, making you think something bad's going to happen, something bad's gonna happen, something bad's gonna happen, then nothing happens. And then more something bad's gonna happen, something bad's gonna happen, something bad's gonna happen and you think no it won't happen because it didn't happen last time then (*Bang.*) it does happen and then there's a dead baby boy and it's all very sad and it's her funeral, er cemetery and there's the tiny brother of the boy, same in *Walk the Line*, the same, very same thing, one boy dead, the other one doesn't know what to do, the parents blame the boy, the boy doesn't blame the parents, everybody fucked, gives a good story, make pop music. Set up – start with something big , blood coming out the door, a man stabbed next two hours you are obliged to stay and watch to find out why the fuck it happened, 'cos you can't go home without this knowledge, you can't rest, you'll never be able to sleep, like the name of some pop star that wrote some pop song that's going around in your head – sign your name across my heart, I want you to be my baby – I'm sick of fucking films. I'm supposed to be on holiday here… Tension, tension tension, it's unbearable, stories, writers, artists. Terence Trent d'Arby.

Pause.

Artists are all fucked up. The better the artist the more fucked up they are. So you're saying to me 'I'm fucked up, I've got good stories for you'?

MARTIN: No.

STEFAN: You're not fucked up? You had two people die in your flat and you're not fucked up?

MARTIN: That's your judgment.

STEFAN: What? So you're normal?

MARTIN: What's normal? Are you normal?

STEFAN: Yeah.

MARTIN: Yeah?

STEFAN: What's not normal about me? What's so weird about me, huh? I wear the clothes.

MARTIN: Just take a look, okay?

STEFAN: Yeah. Where? In the mirror?

MARTIN: No. Not at your reflection.

STEFAN: What? At my soul?

MARTIN: Look at you, look at your life. You think it's normal?

STEFAN: Yeah, you see this is why I, er, you know, this is why I come.

MARTIN: You come?

STEFAN: Yeah, in every sense of the word because it gives me highpoint.

MARTIN: I know, you need to get er what you call it –

STEFAN: Connected, yeah the rest of the life is…yeah I just spend totally up in the head, totally cerebral.

MARTIN: It's good, get fucked, on poppers, why not? You ever been fist-fucked? It's even better, you get really connected then, I'm sure you have, no?

STEFAN: I had er not a real fist, just a little rubber thing, it was more manageable, it was good.

MARTIN: You should go for the real thing, I know a guy who'll do it for free.

STEFAN: Has he got small hands?

MARTIN: Hmm?

STEFAN: Has he got small hands?

MARTIN: No.

STEFAN: Delicate.

MARTIN: Quite big. You want small?

STEFAN: Yeah, I don't think my arse could take it.

MARTIN: Oh, okay.

STEFAN: I haven't got that same strength, you know.

MARTIN: There's another guy here into torture and crucifixion.

STEFAN: What? On the cross?

MARTIN: You go there, ties you up, sticks the nails in – actually I don't know, never tried, but if you want to get connected get in touch with him, get crucified, get fist-fucked –

STEFAN: See, compared to my time in Hamburg –

MARTIN: Poppers.

STEFAN: – it's really fucking boring.

MARTIN: Really, I'm sure.

STEFAN: Yeah, nothing is real compared to this, nothing is real. I delete the history of pages on my internet all the time so my wife can't see the sites I've been on – though one day she was on – I saw this 'cos when I was deleting it later – she was looking for 'www.gardening.com' – things about what to plant, she gets as far as 'G-A' and the url bar pops up six thousand gay sites I've been on. You can't delete it – gay.com, gaydar.com – so she knows, but she chooses not to know.

MARTIN: So you're jealous?

STEFAN: Yes I am, I suppose I am.

MARTIN: Oh.

STEFAN: Yeah, you like that, do you? You and your amazing story.

MARTIN: I didn't say it was amazing.

STEFAN: So why do you want to tell it? What so important? Why not have the story, that's your life, yeah? So you've had the story, you've enjoyed the life, you've enjoyed the moment, now why do you have to tell the story? Why can't you just say 'That was my life. That's how life was'?

MARTIN: Because you have a story, you want it told, but you don't know why.

STEFAN: I'm asking you why.

MARTIN: I'm saying I don't know.

STEFAN: You don't know? So the answer is you don't know why.

MARTIN: Well, it's not just me, it's everyone.

STEFAN: Yeah, everyone wants me me me me, fucking me, yeah… I'm going to have five minutes now of me time.

MARTIN: You are? Now?

STEFAN: No, I'm talking as if I was you.

MARTIN: Me?

STEFAN: Well, you'd be saying 'You you you…', well, no… 'Me me me me me', chairman fucking me.

MARTIN: Nobody knows why.

STEFAN: But I don't ask you – I'm not going around saying I've got great stories.

MARTIN: Because you haven't.

STEFAN: I have got great stories.

MARTIN: And you don't want people to know?

STEFAN: I don't feel the need to tell everybody this is me, aren't I great? But you do.

MARTIN: I did not say aren't I great? I did not say that.

STEFAN: Well, aren't I interesting, then?

MARTIN: Didn't say that.

STEFAN: Okay isn't this story interesting, that happens to me, yeah.

MARTIN: I think it is.

STEFAN: Well then you are different from me.

MARTIN: Who said that?

STEFAN: I said it now.

MARTIN: Well of course I'm different from you.

STEFAN: And you are different from most people.

MARTIN: We are all different from each other, no?

STEFAN: No, because most people don't want to be saying their life story to [some stranger in a bath tub] –

MARTIN: My mother was a prostitute.

STEFAN: Was she?

MARTIN: How about that?

STEFAN: Good, yeah, start from there.

MARTIN: When she was eighteen she went to the next
village and there she would fuck around like hell. Every
week I would see different faces of these Russian guys.
And I know that because I used to get Russian candies
and cookies, a lot, and everything and she always kept
one picture, framed, of this Russian guy. So my father
probably a Russian officer. Never met, never met… Of
course, at school I was always the ugly guy, poor clothes,
crazy haircut, no money, had to steal from my classmates
just to get a bit of bread and margarine… Very, very bad
time. Tough time, nice time. But accidentally I survived.
At high school the teacher drove me crazy. One day I ran
out of the classroom, tried to throw myself off balcony.
She ran after me, pulled me back by the foot and hit me,
buh buh buh buh buh you stupid child… I said to my
sister, whatever you do don't tell our mother, but within
a few days the whole town knew. My mother never said
anything, until one day I was leaving for school she
shouted after me: 'Why didn't you jump? Then I wouldn't
have any problem with you any more…' This incident
followed me to dormitory school. Of course, I never had
Christmas or birthday, never had, but at Christmas I used
to lie to my classmates, yes I've got many presents, but at
home, birthday huh? Many many presents. And Christmas
holiday comes, I go home three hundred kilometers on
the train, get there, there's a note on the door. My mother
has moved to a new town. Four hundred kilometers away.
The caretaker comes to the door with my things in a bag,
says Martin you have to go. I didn't know what to do. I
sit on the train, and I cried, like hell. I got there, walked
down the street, looked around, at the houses, through the
windows, everywhere big family party… My own mother
kicked me out, on Christmas day… Nobody took care…
My sister said to me problem is our mother couldn't love

us because we didn't love her. Actually I feel very pity
for her because she was just a silly uneducated woman,
probably with no love of her own. But I complain to her
many times: it's one thing to fuck someone, it's another
thing to have a child. If you fuck it's fine, but don't raise
the baby if you cannot do that.

Pause.

MARTIN grabs STEFAN's notebook. They wrestle with it.

Let me read it.

STEFAN: No.

MARTIN: You read it, go on.

STEFAN: They're old ideas, nothing to do with this.

MARTIN: You've nothing to hide – read it.

STEFAN: All right. Give it to me and I will.

STEFAN takes it back.

Bangkok Boys Confidential by Sven Deichmann.

MARTIN: Gazman.

STEFAN: Okay. Blah blah blah, I'll just jump in somewhere –
here – 'He's hot now. Tan grinned, but he knew that Sven
needed more stimulation. Raising his elegant palm he
whipped it down and landed smack on one of Martin's butt
cheeks. Martin gagged on Nut's cock filling his mouth as
he felt the sharp pain of that blow on his ass. At the same
time his asshole twitched and gaped open to allow one
of Tan's probing fingers to slide past the ring of defence.
Sven would have yelled at the intense pain but he couldn't
because he had Nut's pecker in his mouth. As several more
open-handed whacks to his butt shocked him in quick
succession Sven's asshole responded. It clamped down
then opened up around the finger digging deep inside
him. There was an unbearable ache and then a burning
sensation. It spread out from his tortured asshole and
slapped ass cheeks into his balls and then directly up his
suddenly fence-post-stiff cock. He almost wept as intense

emotion overwhelmed him. He was either in heaven or hell. "Yeah that's it open up that hot butthole," Tan ordered in his snapping voice. He grunted as he felt Martin's anal lips expand.'

MARTIN: Okay, stop.

STEFAN: '…and his ass thrust back onto his finger. Tan could no longer hold back.'

MARTIN: That's enough.

STEFAN: Wait. Alright but let me do the end bit. 'Sven squirmed a little as the butt plug slid into his ass. "I'm not gay at all," groaned Martin with a smile.' I mean Sven, but you know that it's Martin. Look… I like your story and I think soon you know I want to hear another one but maybe not from you. I met this guy from Uganda who had his ears cut off because he refused to kill his mother or father – so I think I'm going to go with that. It's got a better structure. Simpler. Fits the formula. So I think now I probably go for a walk and maybe party, I have a party or something. Maybe I go to the shops, I could go to the cinema, and maybe read the paper, read a book. Just to fill my hours before I die. So that then I don't have to think about anything. I just – I live, I live, I live, I live, I die. And oooh. Did my life mean anything? Did it mean anything? Do I – you know am I significant? I'm not, I'm totally irrelevant. I think you know I want to eat something now so –

MARTIN: I was in Vietnam with Gary Glitter. You heard this guy?

STEFAN: Yeah?

MARTIN: Yeah, famous. He said 'You wanna meet some boys?'

STEFAN: I thought he was into girls.

MARTIN: Boys, girls, grannies…went to this place –

STEFAN: Look, I want to go to a Thai restaurant. I think take away, and I want to get a Tom Kha, you know, soup, and get out.

MARTIN: Tom Kha?

STEFAN: Like spicy lemongrass.

MARTIN: Oh.

STEFAN: And er tofu, and er bamboo shoots, and er…you know the –

MARTIN: Tom Tam?

STEFAN: Tom Pum?

MARTIN: Tom Tam –

STEFAN: Tom Kha Ja.

MARTIN: Ha ha.

STEFAN: Oh, just a fucking soup with coconut and lemon, you know the thing. The big bowl of soup, yeah. So I thank you and maybe we see us around. Tschus.

MARTIN: Wait…Wait.

The End.